Teddy Bears for Tea

A Book of Poems for Children

Dr. Diana Prince

AuthorHouse™
1663 Liberty Drive
Bloomington, IN 47403
www.authorhouse.com
Phone: 1 (800) 839-8640

Cover and Interior Photos: Used with permission of Getty Images

Published by AuthorHouse 10/26/2016

ISBN: 978-1-5246-4729-2 (sc)
978-1-5246-4730-8 (hc)

Library of Congress Control Number: 2016917846

Print information available on the last page.

This book is printed on acid-free paper.

authorHOUSE®

Teddy Bears for Tea

TABLE OF CONTENTS

THE DOLL HOUSE

The inside walls were shiny tin
With tiny doors to let me in.

The windows had a special place
Where painted roses climbed like lace.

And little dolls placed in a line
Were all dressed up like valentines.

The tiny chairs in my small house
Were small enough to fit a mouse.

And tiny clothes on tiny hooks
Stood by a little shelf of books.

I never could fit in myself
Unless I were a little elf.

Inside, the smallest family
Would wait for me, and count on me.

And after school and in between,
I kept the small rooms neat and clean.

I stacked their shelves with tiny cans,
And washed up all the pots and pans.

I tidied toys into a box
And lined up all their shoes and socks.

Now I am grown and very changed
And all their rooms are rearranged.

Would they still remember me
If I stopped by someday for tea?

THE RAIN

The leaves are spattered dark until they shine,
I buckle up my boots and rush outside

To splash in silver puddles everyplace
And in bright puddles, looking down, I see my face.

The drops on windows cling like little lights,
And I will sleep so sound this rainy night.

But for right now upon my lips, I taste the rain
And watch drops glitter on the windowpane.

On days like this, the beauty makes you cry

When God is dropping diamonds from the sky.

SHOPPING WITH GRANDMA

She fills the bag with apples,
The shiny red that glows,
And tiny little green ones–
(She says the elves grow those.)

She says I'm such a lot of help,
I give her good advice:
"That watermelon looks just right."
"More peaches would be nice."

Today they had some lemonade
With samples from the store
In such tiny paper cups–
I had to ask for more.

We fill the plastic bag with nuts.
We never can decide–
The peanuts or pistachios,
We throw them all inside.

When we get home and stop to rest,
She hands me something new.
I peer inside, she whispers low,
"These peaches are for you."

RABBIT

Billy got an Easter rabbit
In a basket on the floor.

He munched away on carrots
And then expected more.

A few weeks later Billy came
Up to the kitchen door–

He told his mother something
He had never known before,

"That was a magic rabbit,
Cause we now have three or four."

WHAT COLOR IS THE RAIN?

When we see rain clouds slowly pass
They spatter green into the grass.

When we drive back from town
It turn the rooftops sparrow brown.

And the clear drops that we can see
Deepen the green in every tree.

How can a drop so clear as day
Carry each color on its way.

The rain, when sunset comes, I think
Must be a cotton-candy pink.

FLEA MARKET

When they are done with work and play,
The fleas line up for shopping day.

They walk in lines like a parade
To markets set in leafy glades.

Their special day out brings them smiles
While pushing carts down little aisles.

They shop from shelves we cannot see
To buy their cookies and their tea.

They look for bargains, fruits and spice
And sort by color, size and price.

The cakes and cans with little tags
Are added up and put in bags.

Then home they go, where there will be
A festive feast to fit a flea.

PLANTING WITH DAD

We had a million tiny seeds
We carried in a tin.
We made round holes along the wall
And then we dropped them in.

It seems that was so long ago,
Today I had to stare.
I walked outside and spring had brought
Spring flowers everywhere.

BEACH CASTLE

At the beach I built a castle
Made of sand and sea,

A seagull strutted by to watch
And keep an eye on me.

I made the towers higher still
With windows opened high–

A Princess Room to overlook
Young princes riding by.

A curious crab crawled to the door
When all the work was done,

And fell asleep and quickly claimed
My castle in the sun.

TEDDY BEARS AT SCHOOL

Even the smallest of the bears–
This is a general rule–
Will grab their pens and papers
And will love to go to school.

At recess time they laugh and play
And tell the stories that they saved–
And do not yell or push or shove
Because these bears are well-behaved.

At noon they take out sandwiches
Their Mama bears have made,
And sit at little tables
And eat lunches in the shade.

And after taking little naps
Teacher will read aloud,
And if they can recite it back,
It makes them very proud.

And how they love their story time
And all the things they've heard,
They open up their little books
And listen to each word.

EVERY CLOUD IS DIFFERENT

Every cloud is different,
Uncluttered, clean as rain,
Or busy clusters high above
The streak of silver planes.

Some clouds catch on the windows
And on the window sills,
And some clouds are like giants
Resting on the hills.

On other days the clouds will settle
Softly in the air,
Then streams of clouds unravel
Like a mermaid's pale hair.

AUNT BESSIE'S HATS

Aunt Bessie has a hundred hats
Enough to even scare her cats.

One has a rainbow's colored rings;
One has a bird that really sings.

And one with ribbons all around
Aunt Bessie wears to go to town.

My friend and I will stay for hours
And wear the ones with pearls and flowers.

Sometimes we try on every hat,
Sometimes, we simply sit and chat.

There's one hat with a little elf
That always sits upon her shelf.

One with a tiny Eiffel Tower
And tiny mushrooms made of flowers.

Sometimes we wear them and agree
That all our dolls should come to tea.

THE COWBOY

To be a cowboy now of course
I'd probably need to get a horse.

To ride the hills as the sun goes down,
I'd need some boots and a saddle down.

And nothing would stop me after that
As long as I got a cowboy hat.

VISITING AUNTIE ANN

At Auntie Ann's we sit up straight,
And finish what is on our plate.

We sit in chairs with little lace
And doilies put in every place.

And never rush at lunch to eat,
And never wiggle in our seat.

It almost makes me fall asleep
To have so many rules to keep.

Don't drag in mud, don't feed the cat,
Don't put your feet on this or that.

We wash our hands, tuck in our shirt,
I'd rather have a little dirt.

FISHING WITH DAD

We get down to the fishing pier
Before the sun comes up,
And have some toast and maybe
Some chocolate in a cup.

The fish are not awake yet
So we sort the hooks and bait.
And then drop down our fishing lines,
And then we wait and wait.

The sun comes finally overhead,
Just like a golden dish,
And I am like a king today–
In charge of all the fish.

CHURCH VISIT

We stopped to visit God that day
When we walked into town.
We entered through the wooden doors,
My Mom and I knelt down.

He has a lot of windows
That make rainbows in the room,
And lots of roses everywhere
In big red puffy blooms.

We were the only ones inside–
Mom said that wasn't true,
And though we couldn't see them,
There were angels in there, too.

I even prayed for my friend Paul
Who pushed me down and hid,
Mom said that it might
Even make him nicer if I did.

The world's so large God must get tired
Taking good care of it.
But still I'm pretty sure
He saw the candle that we lit.

He must have known I dropped my dime
Into the little cup,
We left without a sound
So that we wouldn't wake Him up.

TEDDY BEARS FOR TEA

In April when it's time for tea,
We set the table neath the tree.

And in the leafy maple's shade
Fill little cups with lemonade.

And then we help our teddy bears
Find just the perfect thing to wear.

With plates of cookies and some milk
And tablecloths of real silk,

And everything that there should be,
Today when Teddies come for tea.

SNAIL THOUGHTS

Why do the snails come out in rain–
In single lines like little trains,
Why do the snails come out in rain?

They crawl along in silver tracks
Each, with a treasure on his back,
is carrying his little house,

And every house the same!

THE PET MOUSE

My little brother found a mouse
That wandered in our yard,
He and my cousin caught it
And they named the mouse "Girard".

The made a little wooden cage
And tied the door with string,
And brought him nuts and apples
But he wouldn't eat a thing.

And then we put some corn flakes
With a napkin underneath,
And we could hear him munching
With his little mousy teeth.

We took him for a bike ride,
I think he fell asleep.
He didn't do a thing.
We had no luck with hide and seek.

We let him go and said goodbye.
The day was almost through.
You'll find there aren't a lot of things
A mouse will like to do.

NEW BABY LAMB

"We'll get a little baby lamb.
Just any day now," Grandpa said.
So I have waited quite awhile,
And think that I will name him Fred.

A few days later, when I checked,
"When will we ever get that lamb?"
"God's working on it. Soon!"
I said, "I'm going to name him Sam."

Imagine when I saw him there
All fluffy white and new.
But God had left already–
So I couldn't thank Him, too.

GOING TO SLEEP

I kissed my Mom
My prayers are said,
I slip away
To go to bed.

Sheets smell like sun
Around my head.
My dog sinks down
Beside my bed.

He's tired as me
Asleep as soon–
Goodnight to stars
And Mr. Moon.

THE SECRET LIFE OF TEDDY BEARS

Today he sits on the windowsill,
And quite content and quiet and still,

But could it be when I'm away
He finds new ways to fill his day?

And does he sail to ancient lands
And cross the desert's golden sands?

Or wander with his little friends
To where the perfect rainbow ends?

There may be signs I might have missed.
Of course, I have no proof of this.

But he is in his favorite chair
When I come home to find him there.

And does he sit there, small and still,
And are his mornings hard to fill?

Things are not always what they seem.
What does he dream of when he dreams?

CHRISTMAS COOKIES

I help bake Christmas cookies
When Christmas time is near,
The Christmas tree's already up,
The snow's already here.

We get out stirring bowls to mix;
And put on aprons when we start,
And take out sugar, and some flour.
My mother says that "It's an art."

It takes all day to do it right
And it's a lot of work and care–
And all the while my brother sits
And watches from his little chair.

The baking is for grown-up kids.
You can't go too fast, or too slow,
And when you do the chocolate chips
You have to get the chips "just so".

We take the flaky coconut
Rolled into round balls as we go,
And then they make some macaroons
That look like little puffs of snow.

We fill the table with the plates
But if my little brother's near
The brand new cookies–one by one
Just seem to disappear.

AT THE MOVIE THEATER

When we go in
To find our seats
Dad asks us
What we want to eat.

Mom gets a coke
And candy drops,
And Dad gets popcorn
In a box.

I get a little box of pez
"Nothing for me," my sister says.

We take our seats,
The movie starts,
And every time,
I don't know how,

That's when I hear my sister say,
"I think I'd like some popcorn now."

JUMPING IN PUDDLES

How many puddles
Would a boy find
On a rainy day
At quarter to nine?

Little John set out,
No umbrella at all,
To find each one
And he found them all.

THE MAGIC OF BOOKS

I took down a book,
And I traveled away
To a land where dolphins
Splash and play.

And rode through the jungle
Just for fun,
Where elephants stood
In the morning sun.

And over a lake
The birds flew by,
Lifting their wings
In the morning sky.

In a book you can
Travel anywhere
And never leave
Your favorite chair.

Go anywhere
You want to be,
And then get home
In time for tea.

PACKING THE CAR FOR VACATION

Vacations are to go and rest,
We thought the dog should maybe come–
He's pretty busy every day,
And tired as everyone.

And then the bird was looking sad
And watched us from afar,
'Till finally we grabbed her cage
And put her in the car.

We would have left the fish behind,
But then it was our wish
To give him more excitement
Than just living in a dish.

Then we climbed in and waited,
For Mom and Dad to come,

Dad came outside, "What's all of this!"
Was all that he could say,
And if you knew My Dad, you'd know
It wasn't in a "good" way.

The suitcases were sitting there
And there was such a fuss–
And for some reason, unexplained,
There wasn't room for us.

ON A PLANE TO SEE GRANDMA

We went to spend Christmas with grandma
In her own little house on a hill
And we flew in a plane over Texas
Under starry skies shiny and still.

In the big cozy plane to see Grandma
I had one thing on my mind,
I thought Santa might just forget us,
And the home we had just left behind.

I had left him some chocolate and cookies
And a note to say I had been good,
And I hoped that he'd leave something special,
And a doll would be nice, if he could.

So Christmas was past by a day and an hour
When we finally flew home in the sky.
And I rubbed my eyes to be certain about
What I saw in the blink of an eye.

As I looked out the big airplane window,
And sat there as still as a mouse,
Santa with all of his reindeer
Were heading straight for our house.

THE TOY TRAIN

It was the best of Christmas gifts,
This little train on tracks
That travelled from the living room
To patio and back.

And all the while it puffed out smoke
And as it made its way
Beyond the TV and the couch
Where pillow mountains lay,

Mother saw Billy quite upset,
"Won't Daddy play? What is it, dear?"

"He'll only play," said Billy then,
"If he can be the engineer."

SUMMER BOAT RIDE

We untie from the pier
And set our white boat free,
We pass the floating buoys
And head out to the sea.

Onshore we see kites fly above
The sandy beaches that we love.

When Dad turns the motor up
To carry us across the bay,
The water flies behind us
In a streak of silver spray.

We have our sandwiches
And little sodas packed in ice,
And take the watermelon out
And have a juicy slice.

The day is crisp, the water blue
And every moment bright and new.

Each sight is new beyond each bend.
We never want the day to end.

PAPER BOAT

Maybe this tiny paper boat
Will travel to a far-off land
Down streams and oceans far away
To land upon some foreign strand.

Maybe this tiny paper boat
Will pass a palace full of light
And see a princess dancing
Under the stars at night.

Or maybe under moonlit fields
Or in a place where magic brings
The sound of fairy laughter
And the flutter of their wings.

Or maybe far beyond this place
Going to school one day,
Some little boy will stop and say
"Who sent this ship so far away?"

TAKING ROVER FOR A RIDE

When we take Rover for a drive
His tail wags and wags.
He sticks his head out for the ride–
His ears wave back like little flags.

He will not leave his window seat,
He will not move or bend–
And all the while his golden fur
Is flying in the wind.

Printed in the United States
By Bookmasters